ANIMAL LIFE STORIES

THE TIGER

Kingfisher Books, Grisewood & Dempsey Ltd,
Elsley House, 24–30 Great Titchfield Street,
London W1P 7AD.

First published in this edition in 1988
by Kingfisher Books.
Some of the illustrations in this book are
taken from *Wildlife Library: The Tiger*
originally published in hardback in 1978.
Reprinted 1988
Copyright © Grisewood & Dempsey Ltd, 1988

BRITISH LIBRARY CATALOGUING IN PUBLICATION DATA
Royston, Angela
    The tiger. – (Picture Kingfisher). –
(Animal life stories).
    1. Tigers – Juvenile literature
    I. Title   II. Series
    599.74'428   QL737.C23
ISBN 0 86272 359 0

Edited by Jacqui Bailey
Designed by Ben White
Cover design by David Jefferis
Cover illustration by Steve Holden/*John Martin &
Artists Ltd*
Phototypeset by Southern Positives & Negatives (SPAN),
Lingfield, Surrey
Printed in Spain

ANIMAL LIFE STORIES

THE TIGER

By Angela Royston
Illustrated by Graham Allen

Kingfisher Books

It is dawn in the forest. In a clearing a deer is grazing. It does not know that in the tall grass nearby a female tiger watches and waits. Slowly the tigress moves closer. She makes no sound, not even stirring the long grass. The deer lifts its head, but it is too late.

5

The tigress pounces. She knocks the deer down and kills it with one bite. Then she eats hungrily. This is her first meal in four days.

When she has eaten enough the tigress rests in a patch of cool shade. Suddenly she pricks up her ears as she hears a roar in the trees close by. She roars back and out of the bushes comes another tiger.

The second tiger is a male. He is bigger than the tigress and his body is long and heavy. At first he is careful not to get too close in case she attacks him, but the tigress wants a mate and she lets him stay.

8

For some days the tigers stay together, hunting and resting and wading in the river to keep cool. One morning another male tiger appears. The tigress's mate roars loudly to tell him to keep away.

One day the tiger pads off into the forest. The tigress will not see him again. When it is nearly time for her cubs to be born, she walks and walks until she finds the right place. It is a dry cave.

For the next few days the tigress stays close to the cave. She hunts a lot, for when her cubs arrive she will not be able to leave them to find food. One night three small cubs are born. They have their eyes tightly shut.

After two weeks the cubs open their eyes and begin to explore their cave home. Their mother has been feeding them on her milk, but she is now hungry and thin. She has to leave them to hunt. She is so tired she does not notice the wild dogs prowling nearby. One dog sneaks into the cave.

Two of the cubs are asleep and well hidden, but the third is awake and is trying to find the way out. The dog carries it away, and when the tigress returns from her hunt she finds only two cubs.

She does not rest but takes the cubs in her mouth.
One by one she carries them to a patch of tall thick
grass. In this safe hiding place they play happily
and grow bigger and stronger.

One of their favourite games is stalking. One cub creeps up and pounces on the other. Then they pounce on their mother's long swishing tail. These stalking games help them learn how to hunt.

One evening when the tigress and her cubs are walking in the forest, they see a huge buffalo. The cubs stay well back as their mother stalks and then pounces on it. But the buffalo is too strong for her. It hits her shoulder with its horns and the tigress falls to the ground. The blow was a hard one, but luckily she is not badly hurt.

As the months go by the cubs join their mother when she hunts. Sometimes she knocks an animal down and stands back to let the cubs finish the kill. Slowly, they are learning to be good hunters.

When the cubs are a year old, the bigger one goes off to hunt alone one night. He crouches quietly at a spot by the river and soon a family of wild pigs come to drink. The young tiger springs and makes his first kill.

The cub carefully drags the pig to some bushes to hide his kill from hungry vultures. Then he fetches his mother and sister to share his meal. A year later both the cubs are ready to leave their mother and she is ready to mate again. Soon she will have new cubs to look after in the forest.

More About Tigers

The tiger is the largest member of the cat family. A fully-grown male tiger may be as long from nose to tail as a four-seater car. Its beautiful black and orange striped coat helps it to hide among the shadows in its forest or grassland home. Tigers are excellent hunters and kill mainly deer, pigs and antelopes, although they will sometimes catch fish.

This sabre-toothed tiger lived about 10,000 years ago. It used its huge dagger-like teeth to kill its prey.

Many people think that tigers live in Africa, but they all live in different parts of Asia. The biggest tigers live in cold Siberia and northern China. The tiger in this story is an Indian tiger.

Ears: Very good hearing. Tigers can hear other animals a long way off

Eyes: Weak. Tigers only see things well when they are close to them

Stripes: These make the tiger harder to see in tall grass, bushes or shadows

Nose: Very good sense of smell

Whiskers: Used to feel their way, especially in the dark

Teeth: The large fangs kill prey and the sharp back teeth chew it up

Some Special Words

Cub A baby or young tiger.

Litter A group of cubs born together. Tigers usually give birth to two or three cubs at a time.

Man-eating tigers Some tigers do eat people, especially in India. Usually though they keep away from people and only attack when they are old or injured and cannot catch their usual prey.

Prey An animal which is hunted and killed for food by another animal.

Stalking The tiger stalks its prey by creeping slowly and silently towards it until it is near enough to pounce. It makes sure that the wind is blowing its own scent away from the other animal.

Tigress A female tiger. She is slightly smaller than male tigers.